TALLEY'S FOLLY

———

By the same author

TALLEY'S FOLLY

A PLAY BY
LANFORD WILSON

A MERMAID DRAMABOOK

 THE NOONDAY PRESS NEW YORK

FARRAR, STRAUS AND GIROUX

For Harold Clurman

Copyright © 1979 by Lanford Wilson
All rights reserved
Published simultaneously in Canada
by McGraw-Hill Ryerson Ltd., Toronto
Printed in the United States of America

Noonday Press edition, 1988
Eleventh printing, 1989

Library of Congress Cataloging in Publication Data

Wilson, Lanford.
Talley's folly.
(A Mermaid dramabook)
I. Title.
PS3573.I458T3   1980   812'.5'4   79–23587
ISBN 0-8090-9128-3
ISBN 0-374-52157-3

TALLEY'S
FOLLY

———

Talley's Folly was first presented by the Circle Repertory Company, in New York City, on May 3, 1979.

Director / Marshall W. Mason
Setting / John Lee Beatty
Costumes / Jennifer Von Mayrhauser
Lighting / Dennis Parichy
Sound / Chuck London
Production Stage Manager / Fred Reinglas

The cast, in order of appearance, was as follows:
MATT FRIEDMAN / Judd Hirsch
SALLY TALLEY / Trish Hawkins

PLACE

An old boathouse on the Talley place,
a farm near Lebanon, Missouri

TIME

July 4, 1944
Early evening

Talley's Folly is to be played without intermission

A Victorian boathouse constructed of louvers, lattice in decorative panels, and a good deal of Gothic Revival gingerbread. The riverside is open to the audience. The interior and exterior walls have faded to a pale gray. The boathouse is covered by a heavy canopy of maple and surrounded by almost waist-high weeds and the slender, perfectly vertical limbs of a weeping willow. Lighting and sound should be very romantic: the sunset at the opening, later the moonlight, slant through gaps in the ceiling and walls reflecting the river in lambent ripples across the inside of the room.

The boathouse contains two boats, one turned upside down, buckets, boxes, no conventional seating. Overhead is a lattice-work attic in which is stored creels, bamboo poles, nets, seines, minnow buckets, traps, floats, etc., all long past use.

At opening: All this is seen in a blank white work light; the artificiality of the theatrical set quite apparent. The houselights are up.

MATT: (*Enters in front of the stage.* MATT FRIEDMAN *is forty-two, dark, and rather large. Warm and unhurried, he has a definite talent for mimicry. In his voice there is still a trace of a German-Jewish accent, of which he is probably unaware. He speaks to the audience*) They tell me that we have ninety-seven minutes here tonight—without intermission. So if that means anything to anybody; if you think you'll need a drink of water or anything . . .

You know, a year ago I drove Sally home from a dance; and while we were standing on the porch up at the house, we looked down to the river and saw this silver flying thing rise straight up and zip off. We came running down to the river, we thought the Japanese had landed some amazing new flying machine, but all we found was the boathouse here, and—uh, that was enough.

3

I'll just point out some of the facilities till everybody gets settled in. If everything goes well for me tonight, this should be a waltz, one-two-three, one-two-three; a no-holds-barred romantic story, and since I'm not a romantic type, I'm going to need the whole valentine here to help me: the woods, the willows, the vines, the moonlight, the band—there's a band that plays tonight, over in the park. The trees, the berries, the breeze, the sounds: water and crickets, frogs, dogs, the light, the bees, working all night.

Did you know that? Bees work—worker bees—work around the clock. Never stop. Collecting nectar, or pollen, whatever a bee collects. Of course their life expectancy is twenty days. Or, in a bee's case, twenty days and twenty nights. Or possibly "expectancy" is wrong in the case of a bee. Who knows what a bee expects. But whatever time there is in a life is a lifetime, and I imagine after twenty days and twenty nights a bee is more or less ready to tuck it in.

(*In a craggy, Western, "Old-Timer" voice*) "I been flyin' now, young sprout, nigh-on to nineteen days an' nineteen nights."

(*Imitating a young bee*) "Really, Grandpa Worker Bee?"

(*Old-Timer*) "An' I'm 'bout ready to tuck it in."

(*Slight pause. Reflectively*) Work. Work is very much to the point. (*Showing the set*) We have everything to help me here. There's a rotating gismo in the footlights (do you believe footlights) because we needed the moon out there on the water. The water runs right through here, so you're all out in the river—sorry about that. They promise me moonlight by the baleful, all through the shutters. We could do it on a couple of folding chairs, but it isn't bare, it isn't bombed out, it's rundown, and the difference is all the difference. And valentines need frou-frou.

We have a genuine Victorian folly here. A boathouse. Constructed of louvers, and lattice and geegaws. I feel like a real-estate salesman. Of course there's something about the term "real estate" that strikes me as wrong. Estate maybe, but real is arguable. But to start you off on the right foot . . . Everybody ready? This is a waltz, remember, one-two-three, one-two-three.

There was a time—or, all right, I think that has to be: Once upon a time—there was a hope throughout the land. From the chaos of the Great Depression, people found strength in union, believing their time had come. But even as this hope was perceived, once again a dark power rose up from the chaos in another land. Once again this country pitched its resources and industry into battle. Now, after almost three years of war, it has become apparent that the battle is turning. Once again we are told that "peace and prosperity" are in the air. But in the midst of battle, that "hope" the people had known has been changed into the enemy. Peace, and—more to the point—prosperity, is our ally now. Once again, we are told the country has been saved by war.

Now, you would think that in this remote wood, on this remote and unimportant, but sometimes capricious, river—that world events would not touch this hidden place. But such is not the case. There is a house on the hill up there, and there is a family that is not at peace but in grave danger of prosperity. And there is a girl in the house on the hill up there who is a terrible embarrassment to her family because she remembers that old hope, and questions this new fortune, and questioning eyes are hard to come by nowadays. It's hard to use your peripheral vision when you're being led by the nose.

Now I know what you're thinking. You're saying if I'd known it was going to be like this, I wouldn't have come. Or if I'd known it was going to be like this, I would have listened. But don't worry, we're going to do this first part all over again for the late-comers. I want to give you and me both every opportunity. So. Okeydokey. (*Checks pocket watch*) Oh, boy, this has gotta be fast. So: (*Deep breath, then all in a run*) They tell me that we have ninety-seven minutes here tonight without intermission so if that means anything to anybody if you think you'll need a drink of water or anything I'll just point out some of the facilities till everybody gets settled in if everything goes well for me tonight this should be a waltz one-two-three, one-two-three a no-holds-barred romantic story and since I'm not a romantic type I'm going to need the whole shmeer here to help me the woods the willows the vines the moonlight the band there's a band that plays tonight over in the park the trees the berries the breeze the sounds water and crickets frogs dogs the light the bees . . . (*Pauses. With a slight hill accent*) Frogs, dogs . . . (*To stage manager in sound booth*) Could we have a dog? I'd like a dog. (*He listens a second. Nothing. Then a furious, yapping, tiny terrier is heard*) Fellas! Fellas! A dog! (*Beat. Then a low, distant woof-woof-woof that continues until* SALLY's *entrance.* MATT *listens a beat, pleased*)

Oh, yeah. Old man Barnette kicked out Blackie and called in the kids, and about now the entire family is sitting down to supper. Even Blackie, out by the smokehouse. But a car pulled off the road about a mile downstream, and someone got out. And at this hour it begins to be difficult to see, the chickens have started to go to bed, and noises carry up the river as though there was someone there in the barnyard. And Blackie wants to let everybody know the Barnette farm is well guarded. (*Beat. Then back to run-on narration*)

Working all night did you know that bees work worker bees work around the clock never stop collecting nectar or pollen whatever a bee collects of course their life expectancy is twenty days or in a bee's case twenty days and twenty nights or possibly expectancy is wrong in the case of a bee who knows what a bee expects but whatever time there is in a life is a lifetime and I imagine after twenty days and . . .

SALLY: (*Off, yelling*) Matt? (MATT *is silent. He almost holds his breath*) Matt? (*The houselights begin to dim. The sunset and reflection from the river begin to appear; we hear the sound of the river and birds*) Matt?

MATT: (*Softly, to the audience*) This is a waltz, remember. One-two-three, one-two-three . . .

SALLY: (*Off*) Are you in that boathouse? I'm not going to come down there if you're not there 'cause that place gives me the creeps after dark. Are you down there?

MATT: No.

SALLY: (*Coming closer*) I swear, Matt Friedman, what in the devil do you think you're doing down here? (*Coming through the tall weeds and willow*) Oh, my—everything is soaking wet here. Buddy said he chased you off with a shotgun. I thought, good, we're maybe rid of you. I saw your car parked up there, I could not believe my eyes! (*She enters*) Not even you! And there you sit. Wiping your glasses. (SALLY TALLEY *is thirty-one. Light, thin, quite attractive, but in no way glamorous or glamorized. Straightforward, rather tired, and just now quite angry. In this state she has a pronounced Ozark accent, but when she concentrates on what she is saying, the accent becomes much less pronounced*)

MATT: The better to see you with, my dear.

SALLY: Don't even begin with me, Matt, I'm in no mood.

MATT: Were you hiding behind the window curtains when I was out in the yard talking to your brother? You like to hide from me so much.

SALLY: I got home five minutes ago. You know what time I get off work. Rachel and Ida dropped me out front, we could hear Buddy cussin' all the way out to the road.

MATT: You talk to your Aunt Charlotte? How did you know I'd be here?

SALLY: I was inside that house exactly thirty seconds. I walked in the door, Momma and Buddy lit in on me like I was ten years old, screaming about the Communist traitor infidel I'd let in the house. Buddy said he run you off with a shotgun.

MATT: He had a large two-barreled weapon, yes, with apertures about like so.

SALLY: If they knew you were still on the place, they'd have Cliffy on you.

MATT: You want the sheriff, all you have to do is keep yelling. Your sister-in-law called him. He's probably at your house right now.

7

SALLY: (*Near whisper*) Whatever possessed you to come down here and get into a fight with my brother? You know I can't stand livin' there as it is.

MATT: Sally, one of us had better go for a walk and cool off. Both of us can't be angry.

SALLY: What better happen is you better march right back up there to your car and head back to St. Louis.

MATT: No, see, the way they build those things now they require gasoline to really get them running good. Especially Plymouths.

SALLY: Matt Friedman, you did not run out of gas.

MATT: You want to go try it? See if you can get it to catch?

SALLY: Oh, if that isn't just . . . typical.

MATT: That's what saves it, I think. I was just thinking that that was typical.

SALLY: That car is gonna kill me. I mean, I'm a strong person, but that car is gonna do it. Not one time has that car gone from one place to another place without breaking down.

MATT: Sally, you don't deprecate a man's car. A man's car reflects his pride in himself and his status in society. Castigate my car, you castigate me.

SALLY: Well, good. And you may be full of hot air on most things, but you are right about that. That—that—haybailer!— is a good reflection of you.

MATT: Boy, you get angry, you really are a mountain daughter, aren't you? Where's the still? I was looking for the still you said was down here.

SALLY: Matt, I'm exhausted. I've been up since five. I was at the hospital at six-thirty. I don't want to argue. The still was right there. They busted it up—broke it up.

MATT: Your dad get raided by Cliffy?

8

SALLY: Cliffy wasn't sheriff then, McConklin was sheriff. Him and Dad were half-partners in the still. They broke it up to sell for scrap after the repeal. Matt—

MATT: They were runnin' liquor, were they?

SALLY: Is the only thing keeping you here a gallon of gas for your car? 'Cause we have a can in the pump house.

MATT: Better wait till it gets a little darker if you're gonna start stealing Buddy's gas.

SALLY: You've alienated Buddy. You've almost paralyzed Olive.

MATT: (*Snapping his fingers*) Olive! Olive! I could not think of your sister-in-law's darn name! I'm thinking pickled herring, I'm thinking caviar, I'm thinking boiled egg. I knew she was on a relish tray.

SALLY: Why are you always barging in places?

MATT: No, ma'am. I wrote you how many times I'd be down today.

SALLY: You barge into a person's home, you barge into where they work!

MATT: I telephoned your house here. I had a nice Missouri telephone chat with your Aunt Charlotte.

SALLY: Aunt Lottie would invite the devil into the parlor for hot cocoa.

MATT: Actually, I came here to talk to your father. That's the way I've been told these things are done in the South.

SALLY: You're not in the South. You're in the Midwest.

MATT: Sally, I've been all over the country, and there is New York City, isolated neighborhoods in Boston, and believe me, the rest is all the South.

SALLY: Would you please just tell me what happened up there so I'll know how to handle them?

9

MATT: Sally, I know I told you we'd have the whole weekend, and I've been looking forward to it just as much as you have, but there was—

SALLY: You are the most conceited, blind, deaf—

MATT: —just no way out of it. I have to go back tonight. We have a hearing on the iceman and his horse, there was no way—

SALLY: On what?

MATT: You know, I wrote you, the iceman, with a horse and wagon. We had him consecrated as a church and that worked for two years, till they caught on, but—

SALLY: I don't have any idea what you are talking about.

MATT: (*Going on*)—churches don't pay taxes. We had him ordained. They didn't like it. So we set up a trust fund in the name of Daisy; now they want a hearing on that, because horses can't hold trusts. It was just sprung on us. I have to be back in St. Louis tomorrow.

SALLY: Would you just tell me what happened up there?

MATT: It was crazy to come down here, only I promised you, but we have to work fast here tonight.

SALLY: What was Buddy so mad about?

MATT: Did you hear me? I've only got tonight; I have to get back.

SALLY: Would you please just—

MATT: Sally, it is unimportant, but if it makes you happy! I came down here as I said I would; I parked my car, went to the front door, and knocked. Your sister-in-law—from the relish tray? You said?

SALLY: Olive.

MATT: Olive! I cannot remember the woman's—Olive! Olive! Olive came to the door, with very big eyes, shaking all over. I said, "Oh, hello, I'm Matt Friedman. I thought I'd come over this beautiful evening and have a chat with Mr. Talley." So she stood there doing her imitation of a fish, and—

SALLY: She did what?

MATT: She couldn't speak, I think. She was paralyzed. She goes — (*Imitates a fish*)

SALLY: It isn't necessary to characterize every—

MATT: Sally, I'm trying to tell this in a way that I don't get angry again.

SALLY: Okay!

MATT: Finally she swims off, after having said all of not one word, and Buddy came— Does your entire family have such absurd names?

SALLY: His real name is Kenny. We call him Buddy.

MATT: Kenny? Is his real name? This is better, for a grown man, Kenny? Kenny Talley, Lottie Talley, Timmy Talley, Sally Talley? Your brother also does not know how to converse. Your brother talks in rhetorical questions: "You're Sally's Jewish friend, ain't ya? What do you think you want here? Did you ever hear that trespassing was against the law?"

SALLY: Oh, they're all such hypocrites and fools.

MATT: There was nothing hypocritical about it, believe me.

SALLY: You deserve it, coming down here. I told you Dad said you weren't invited back.

MATT: So Buddy said, If you want to see your friend Sally, you can go to Springfield, where she works, and I said I'd wait there in the yard—and he went in and got a two-barreled hunting gun.

SALLY: And Olive called the sheriff.

MATT: I am omitting the yelling and the screaming and the deprecating.

SALLY: Who was yelling?

MATT: Well, there was your Aunt Charlotte yelling: "This man came to see me." And your mother yelling: "You are not to see my daughter." And Olive yelling, "Get back in the house" at everybody, at Charlotte, at Buddy, at the dog that was barking, at your brother's business friend—who was out in the yard to protect Buddy; he mostly said, "You tell 'em, Buddy, you tell 'em, Buddy." (*Pause*)

SALLY: (*Moves away, turns to him*) I'm not even gonna apologize, you had it coming to you.

MATT: Of course, your mother and Olive stayed up there on the screened-in porch, protected from the mosquitoes and Communists and infidels.

SALLY: (*Turning away*) I have absolutely got to get out of that place. Rachel and Ida and I have been looking for an apartment in town for months.

MATT: (*Watches her. Lightly*) Actually you don't get mosquitoes here, do you? Rich people always know where to build their houses. With the house on the hill, in the breeze, the river always moving, mosquitoes don't nest around here. The breeze blows them off. Do they nest? Mosquitoes? Do mosquitoes nest? Does everything that lays eggs nest? Do fish nest? That's a funny idea.

SALLY: Don't try to make me feel good, Matt, it isn't going to work. Fish spawn.

MATT: What do mosquitoes do?

SALLY: I do not know what mosquitoes do. They breed.

MATT: You know, I'll bet you're right. (*Beat*) See, I thought you'd be glad to see me. That's my problem. I got no sounding board. I sit up there in St. Louis in this dusty office sneezing away, I get to daydreaming. I start thinking: (*Ozark accent*) Well, now, listen here, Matthew, what ort to happen is you ort to head on down into them hills an—

SALLY: Please don't do that. Don't make fun of the way we talk. Oh! Everything you do! You're enough to make a—

MATT: (*Beat*) Preacher cuss. (*Beat*) Sailor blush.

SALLY: I don't make fun of your accent, I don't see why—

MATT: (*With an unconscious but pronounced accent*) I have no accent. I worked very hard and have completely lost any trace of accent.

SALLY: Very well.

MATT: And daydreaming away up there, I said to myself: (*Bogart*) This—un—Sally dame. She—uh—looks to me like a good deal, Matt. She—uh—showed you a good time. The least you could do is reciprocate.

SALLY: That's supposed to be someone, I guess. That isn't you.

MATT: What do you mean, "someone"? You don't know Humphrey Bogart?

SALLY: We don't go to the pictures.

MATT: How did you know he was a movie actor? He might be the Secretary of the Interior; he—

SALLY: My grandmother knows Humphrey Bogart and she's never been to a—

MATT: You don't castigate a guy's imitations, Sal.

SALLY: The Secretary of the Interior has been Harold Ickes since Sitting Bull.

MATT: You don't go to the movies?

SALLY: Pictures are an excuse to sit alone in the dark.

MATT: To sit together in the dark.

SALLY: Not necessarily.

MATT: But you go alone.

SALLY: Not always.

MATT: (*With sexual overtones*) Oh, ho . . . now, that's—interesting.

SALLY: Sometimes with some of the other nurse's aides from work.

MATT: (*After a pause*) That's a big business, isn't it? Caring for the wounded. It's a nice place for the boys to forget about the hard realities of making a buck when they get out.

SALLY: The boys we take care of have seen their share of hard realities.

MATT: It's a very sunny building. The boys all have a very sunny attitude. The doctors are very sunny, the nurses are very sunny, the nurse's aides are sunny. You expect the whole place to go up with spontaneous combustion.

SALLY: We try to be pleasant, yes. What would you have us do? Say, "Oh my gosh, you look horrible, I don't think you're going to make it through the night"? "Good Lord, you poor man, both hands missing and all you know is auto mechanics; you're never going to find a job you're happy with."

MATT: No, I wouldn't have you do—

SALLY: (*Almost angry*) We don't have to fake anything. When you work with them every day you can see progress. Some of them will recover completely.

MATT: I'm not criticizing, I admire it.

SALLY: I was there last February when you barged in, I wasn't home!

MATT: Oh, yes, yes, that was funny. One girl said you had a cold that day, and another girl said you had gone to Kansas City to help requisition more beds. She was very imaginative, but under sympathetic questioning she was not a good fibber.

SALLY: So you drove all that way down to Springfield and all that way back for nothing.

MATT: It wasn't a wasted afternoon. I had the honor to be shown by a Negro private from California twenty-five different ways I can lose the game of checkers. Also, I had time to puzzle. Why would Sally tell every person with whom she works that if this hairy Jewish accountant comes down like a crazy man to see her . . . everybody tell him she's not here and Sally will hide in a closet.

SALLY: I was working in the kitchen that morning, where visitors are not allowed. It was not necessary to hide.

MATT: With little nurses coming into the kitchen every ten minutes to say: "Well, I don't know, Sally, he's still up there. Looks like he intends to stay all day." Puzzles don't waste my time, Sally. I'm very good at puzzles. I have great powers of ratiocination. I'm a regular Sherlock. He was a terrible anti-Semite. He was a rather shallow, ignorant man. Did you know that?

SALLY: I'm sorry, I wasn't listening. I was trying to figure out what "ratiocination" means.

MATT: Oh, forgive me. I don't have a speaking vocabulary. I have a reading vocabulary. I don't talk that much.

SALLY: I haven't noticed the problem.

MATT: Last year, weren't you always saying how quiet I was? Matt, why don't you say something—weren't you always asking me questions?

SALLY: (*Moving toward the door*) I retract everything I said last summer.

MATT: (*Moving to cut her off with rather surprising agility*) But unlike Sherlock Holmes, I'm not quick. I'm steady and I stay at something, but I'm thick. *First*, it took a long time for me to know something as thick as me. And *then*, going back over the mystery of Sally in the closet, I decided what was called for was an on-the-spot investigation.

SALLY: Matt, I'm—

MATT: (*Taking a notepad from his pocket*) So I have a few questions I'd like to put to you.

SALLY: There is no mystery.

MATT: Mystery isn't bad, Sally. Mystery is the spice of life.

SALLY: Variety is the spice of life.

MATT: Well, variety has always been a mystery to me. Give me one choice and I can take it or leave it. Give me two and I can't decide. Give me three, I don't want any of it. Now—

SALLY: I cannot understand why you can't get the message. You sound like a functioning human being; but you've got a wire crossed or something.

MATT: A screw loose.

SALLY: You are one total, living loose screw. That much is certain. You've been away a solid year. The one time you come to the hospital to hunt me down I refuse to see you—

MATT: No, no, you didn't refuse, you hid in the kitchen.

SALLY: And you sat up there in that dayroom the entire blessed afternoon.

MATT: I was not made to feel unwelcome.

SALLY: *Not made to feel unwelcome?* You do not have the perception God gave lettuce. I did not answer but one letter and in that one short note I tried to say in no uncertain terms that I didn't want you to write to me. You have sent me an almost *daily* chronicle of your life in your office. The most mundane details of your accounting life. Why did you come back here?

MATT: It was a very pleasant way to begin the morning: writing, Dear Sal. Cleared out my head, like reading the newspaper, only not so depressing. I could tell you about the intrigue in the office; mull over the problems I anticipated. And knowing you—you sort of spoke along with me. Your carefully balanced and rational judgment was a great boon to my disposition. Improved the weather. And the weather in St. Louis needs all the improvement it can get. I'll bet I made you laugh.

SALLY: No, you did not.

MATT: No?

SALLY: Not once.

MATT: That's a blow.

SALLY: I knew you were trying to, but I didn't find anything particularly funny.

MATT: Not trying. I just thought you might. You didn't get lonely. It wasn't like being away from me this whole year, was it?

SALLY: Not at all.

MATT: Didn't you come to look forward to the mail in the morning?

SALLY: I dreaded each new day.

MATT: Now see, if I believed that, I'd leave.

SALLY: I did gain a fondness for the calm respectability of Sunday.

MATT: Holidays must have been nice.

SALLY: Holidays were a benediction.

MATT: Did you make the recipe I sent you? I couldn't make it because I don't have a timer. Baking in an oven, I forget what I'm doing and I go off and leave. I come back, the apartment is terrible. I cook well—

SALLY: —I don't cook. Why don't you just go on up the road to the Barnettes'? It isn't that far. They'll give you enough gas to get into town.

MATT: You have no sense of nostalgia, Sal. You have no romance.

SALLY: No, I do not. Not right now. I can't remember feeling less romantic.

MATT: Alone. Together again in the sunset—well, sundown—twilight. (*Pause, looks around and out over the river*) This country. I mean, this countryside. Is so beautiful. Do you think about that when you live in it all the time? Surrounded by all this lovely scenery? Or do you take it for granted?

SALLY: We know it's beautiful. Why wouldn't we appreciate it? There has to be some compensation in the place. It isn't particularly fertile; it's rocky; it's got poor drainage; it's all hills.

MATT: How can it have poor drainage if it's all hills?

SALLY: Hills have nothing to do with drainage. Water has to soak into the ground, not run off. The weather is too dry in the summer, the crops just curl up in the field. The spring is nothing but a cycle of floods. The winters are too cold, and damp, and . . .

MATT: But it's beautiful. (*He has been rubbing his hands on a side of the upturned boat. His finger has just jabbed a hole in the side*) Gottenyu! Look at that. That goes right through. Not what I'd call seaworthy. Riverworthy. When was the last time anybody was down here? Aside from you, coming down here to get away from the house? Aside from you and me coming down here last summer?

SALLY: I wouldn't know.

MATT: Ought maybe to fix the place up.

SALLY: Nobody has any use of it any more. You couldn't get materials now if you wanted to.

MATT: Fancy place to let rot away. Nobody even knows who spent all that much time building some crazy place like this. It isn't really grand, it's just silly. Is it not silly? Must have broken a lot of jigsaw blades.

SALLY: Uncle Whistler.

MATT: What?

SALLY: Everett Talley. Built the boathouse in 1870. Built follies all over town. He wanted to build a gazebo up by the house, but Grandpa said it was a frivolity, so he built a boathouse.

MATT: And made it look like a gazebo.

SALLY: Well, that's what he wanted to do in the first place. He did the bandstand in the park across the river. The town didn't want it, but he'd seen it in a picture somewhere so he went over and built it. They tried to stop him, he went right on; said they could tear it down after he had finished. Painted it maroon and pink and gold. Said, "Now, tear it down." Eventually they used it for high school band concerts.

MATT: Sounds like a frustrated guy.

SALLY: Not at all! Why does everything have to be cynical? He was not in the least frustrated. He was a happily married man with seven kids. He made toys. Tap-dancing babies and whirligigs. He got pleasure out of making things for people. He did exactly what he wanted to do. He was the healthiest member of the family. Everybody in town knew him. They all called him Whistler.

MATT: Because he was the artist in the family?

SALLY: Because he sang and whistled. He used to go stomping through the woods singing "*Una furtiva lagrima*" at the top of his lungs; nobody outside the Talleys knew what he was singing, so they all said he was crazy, but he certainly wasn't frustrated.

MATT: (*He has found an ice skate*) What is that? An ice skate? Somebody had big feet. Do you skate?

SALLY: No.

MATT: Me too. Did you use to roller skate on the sidewalk?

SALLY: There isn't a sidewalk closer than a mile and a half, in town.

MATT: Me too. All the other kids had skates. Fly past me, knock me down. I was only five. Some memories linger.

SALLY: In St. Louis?

MATT: (*Beat. He does not answer her*) In the winter they skated on the lake. Frozen solid. I tried another boy's skates on once. Nearly broke my neck. Well, that's what I should have expected. I am not what you would call a beautifully co-ordinated individual.

SALLY: Oh, don't put those on!

MATT: That roller rink in Lebanon where the soldiers all hang out. That's the principal recreation here, it seems.

SALLY: People come up from Springfield.

MATT: Fellas and their dates?

SALLY: Girls looking for soldiers.

MATT: Looks like everybody is having a good time. All that drinking and all that skating, I'd get sick.

SALLY: They do.

MATT: You go?

SALLY: I went once, Matt, I didn't like it. (*He has put the skates on his feet*) Don't stand up in those, you'll go right through the floor.

MATT: No, no, it's all a matter of balance. (*Stands, nearly falls over, grabs the wall*)

SALLY: Don't do that— Oh, for crying out loud.

MATT: Unfortunately, I have almost no sense of balance at all. (*He is holding on*) What do you do? You have to push off to start. Then you glide.

SALLY: You don't have to push off, but I suppose you could.

MATT: Eventually you come to a standstill. How do you keep going?

SALLY: You take steps. Step, push. And you glide on that foot. Your weight on that one foot.

MATT: How do you get your weight off one foot and onto another?

SALLY: The other foot has to come up.

MATT: How can the other foot come up?

SALLY: Lift it! (*She goes to him, pulls at one foot*) Oh, for godsake, lift it!

MATT: (*Unsteady, still holding on to the wall*) Oh . . . One foot.

SALLY: Now, you're gliding on that one foot. Before you start to slow down, you lean your weight over onto the other.

MATT: Oh, sure. What's to catch me if I shift my weight off of this foot?

SALLY: The other foot. You've got two, stupid.

MATT: Sally, I'm awkward, I'm not stupid.

SALLY: Put the *other foot* down! (*He does*)

MATT: (*On both feet again*) That's much easier.

SALLY: Now, lift the other foot.

MATT: I know, I know. And glide on that. (*He has taken hold of her and let go of the wall*) Why don't the skaters get tangled up?

SALLY: Because they're synchronized.

MATT: I'm not going to worry about what you do, okay? You'll confuse me. (*Singing "Over the Waves," waltz-tempo, low at first, gaining in confidence*) La-la-la-la-la-bop-bop-bop—

SALLY: (*For one moment they appear to be skating*) Come on, not so loud.

MATT: La-la-la-la-la-la-la-la-bop-bop-boom-bop-bop—

SALLY: Come on, Matt, stop. They'll hear you across the river.

MATT: I'm having an old-fashioned skate with my girl.

SALLY: I'm not your girl, Matt. Come on. Let go, you're ridiculous.

MATT: Don't let go. Don't let go! We're coming to the end of the pond.

SALLY: (*Has disentangled herself. He is flailing his arms with nothing to hold on to*) I'm going to go get gasoline for your car.

MATT: (*As if heading for the edge of the pond*) I'm going too fast! I don't know how to turn. Sally! I'm gonna crash! Help! The trees are looming up in front of me. They're coming right at me. Fir trees and big old maple trees. Oak trees! They're black against the snow. Firelight flickering on them from the campfire. They're frozen hard as stone and deadly. It's the end of a brilliant career! Here they come. I can't slow down! Here they come! AAAAAAAAaaaaaaaaa! (*Falls down*) Oh, oh . . . I'm in serious— Where are you going? Sally?

SALLY: (*She has stood with her arms crossed, watching him. Now she turns to leave*) I'm going for your gas.

MATT: Sally? Hey, I can't run after you in these.

SALLY: Good. I'm good and sick of you running after me, Matt. (*She is gone*)

MATT: Come on. (*He tries to run after her*) Where do you think you are going— (*As his leg crashes through the floor, he grabs at the overhead lattice. It gives way and falls on him, dumping the reels, creels, baskets, nets, etc., over him*) Oh, my God! Sally? Help. Sally? (*He fights his way clear of the mess to see her standing in the doorway again*) I fell through the floor.

22

SALLY: (*Somewhat concerned*) Where are you hurt? What did you hurt?

MATT: Sally. Come on—uh . . . (*Fends her off a moment*) I appreciate your concern, but—just let me think a second. (*Pause*) Uh, no, in all honesty, I think I'm not injured at all. Except maybe my head. That stuff came down on me. (*Laughs*) Look at you standing there with your arms crossed. (*Tries to rise*) Uh. There's one problem. I don't know how I'm supposed to get out of this. My leg's through the floor. Give me a lift.

SALLY: Oh, good Lord. (*Tries to help*) They must have heard you up to the house; across the river.

MATT: I was having fun. It's very good exercise, skating.

SALLY: (*Giving up*) I can't. You're too big. And you're not helping.

MATT: I'm helping, I'm helping.

SALLY: You'll have to get out by yourself. What a baby.

MATT: It's not so bad here. (*Looking around*) It's not an uncomfortable position. My vanity is a little confused, but outside of that.

SALLY: You're not going to be so comfortable when you get your foot snake-bit.

MATT: Oh, my God. (*He manages to scramble out of the hole*) You know all the right things to say. (*Looking his leg over*) I think I'm not injured. No, I'm not even skinned. The wood is too rotten to scrape me even.

SALLY: You could have scratched yourself on a rusty nail and gotten blood poisoning.

MATT: No, I had a tetanus shot before I came down. That's what you have to get when you go fishing. I read about it. In case you prick your finger with a fish hook. Most painful thing

23

I ever paid to have done to myself. (*Sits, takes off the skates*)
Were you serious about the snakes?

SALLY: Copperheads, water moccasins, cottonmouths. I mean,
they won't prey on you. But I imagine if you stuck your foot
right in their nest, they wouldn't like it.

MATT: Snake's nest? (*He gets up, pushes something over the
hole*) Had you told me about the snakes last year when we
came down here, there would never have been an affair between Sally and Matt. (*Sits again to put his shoes on*)

SALLY: There was no affair.

MATT: Of course there was an affair. How many times in seven
days did I see you?

SALLY: I don't know.

MATT: Seven.

SALLY: Seven.

MATT: Seven. I got hoarse screaming over the music of that
dance band. I could hardly speak all week long.

SALLY: The kids nowadays like it so loud they don't have to
think.

MATT: I don't blame them.

SALLY: Neither do I.

MATT: You didn't mind me talking to you. Out on the porch
of the Shriners' mosque.

SALLY: I didn't mind talking to you; I didn't mind you driving
me home; I didn't even mind changing the tire.

MATT: I thought we made a very good team. Most girls would
have stayed in the car. You at least held the flashlight.

SALLY: *Held the flashlight?*

MATT: Well, and told me how to change the tire.

SALLY: And lit matches so you could see, when the flashlight batteries burned out. I could have done it much faster myself. What I minded was the very next evening walking two miles when the carburetor failed.

MATT: I told you to wait in the car. I told you not to come.

SALLY: What is someone going to say, with me sitting alone in the car on a road where lovers park, where I have never been before in my life. Even during school.

MATT: I tried to hitchhike us a ride; you hid in the bushes every time a car came by. I'm looking around for you, the drivers all think I'm drunk and pull over into the other lane. You almost caused three head-on collisions that night.

SALLY: Aside from that night, the other times I saw you were a lot of fun. Except maybe the night you came to dinner.

MATT: I am not responsible for your family. That evening was your idea.

SALLY: Everyone is always saying what a crazy old-maid Emma Goldman I'm becoming, I wanted to show them how conservative and ignorant I really am.

MATT: You are not conservative, you are not ignorant, and Emma Goldman, believe me, was no old maid.

SALLY: You know what I mean. Between being what they consider out-and-out anti-American and being over forty years old, and having a beard, you made a grand hit with Mom and Dad, let me tell you.

MATT: I could tell.

SALLY: You left the house, Dad said, That man is more dangerous than Roosevelt himself.

MATT: What they were hoping was that I would be a proper Christian suitor and take crazy Sally off their hands.

SALLY: (*She gets up to go*) No, at least they've stopped hoping that. That's something.

MATT: Where are you going? When we're getting on so well.

SALLY: We are not getting on so well.

MATT: (*Manages to get between* SALLY *and the door, blocking her way*) Sally, listen. You're scared and I'm scared, but we both have to realize that we're going to deal with this before either of us leaves.

SALLY: There's nothing to deal with, Matt.

MATT: No, there's quite a lot. We can't have it both ways. You can chase me away or you can put on a pretty dress. But you can't put on a pretty dress to come down here and chase me away. (*Beat*) You remember I've seen you come home from work in your uniform.

SALLY: I changed out of my uniform at work tonight.

MATT: Because you thought I'd meet you in Springfield, outside the hospital.

SALLY: I didn't know you'd be down here; I thought I'd come down here to listen to the band.

MATT: You were coming to the boathouse because this is where we came last year.

SALLY: This is my place. I come down here every day.

MATT: Okay, fine, I'll believe that. You go to the boathouse to forget your family. Maybe you have a cigarette to unwind, knowing you can't smoke up at the house; maybe you take a nip from a whiskey bottle you keep here somewhere.

SALLY: I won't stay up there forever. I'm as eager to leave as they are eager to get rid of me.

MATT: Maybe get an apartment in Springfield. Share with Rachel and Ida, so the three of you don't have to drive to work every morning.

SALLY: They're nice girls.

MATT: They're very nice. Maybe get a pet dog. A dachshund, maybe, name him Matt. Smoke all you want to in your own apartment. Go out to the movies on Saturday night. Maybe go sometimes to the USO dances? Not get too involved with any of the boys, not Sally.

SALLY: Is that bad?

MATT: No, ma'am, it is not. You do real work at the hospital. All the boys said they liked you best. All those other nurses, though, with their eyes they were saying: "Don't you go away, Matt, Sally is gonna come around."

SALLY: They enjoyed the game.

MATT: Yes, me too. But they weren't telling me to go away.

SALLY: Well, then I'm telling you to go away; nothing will come from it, Matt—

MATT: See, they could tell that I was in love with you, and they were telling me you might be in love with me, and wouldn't that be a catastrophe.

SALLY: (*Beat*) I don't think I even know what that means; I don't know if you know what that—

MATT: Aside from that, though, you're afraid you might love me.

SALLY: I don't think *that* is even a desirable state to be in—

MATT: Agreed, a hundred percent; all you have to say is, No, I am not.

SALLY: Why don't you just leave and make us all happier.

MATT: I don't know that leaving would make you happy. It wouldn't make me happier. It would be easier. See, I can take no for an answer; I can't take evasion, I can't take I'm scared, I can't take hiding in the kitchen.

SALLY: Just put it out of your mind, Matt. It's impossible.

27

MATT: So the future is pug dogs and apartments and USO get-togethers and drinking with the girls.

SALLY: It sounds wonderful.

MATT: Sally has decided she is an eccentric old maid, and she is going to be one.

SALLY: I'm looking forward to it.

MATT: (*He sighs. Pause. Gets out a notebook*) Well, see, I'll show you how far Sherlock got. My first solution to the Sally-in-the-closet puzzle—

SALLY: Kitchen.

MATT: Sally hiding in the kitchen—was, she don't want nothing to do with this Jew-type. (*Mild Jewish accent*) It no matter that she never saw one before, she has heard great much about dem. Days alvays beink shased from place to place, must be somethink wrong. Anyvay, *shiksas* are gullible breeds an belief everythink they hear.

SALLY: Oh, you don't think that at all. I'm a liberal Midwestern college graduate. You were very exotic to me. I reread the Old Testament.

MATT: Well, I hate to disillusion you, but I didn't reread the New Testament. (*Tearing off the page of the notebook; throwing it away*) So it is not that. Everything must be in a list for me or I get confused. Then I said maybe the reason Sally is so scared is it's this (*German accent*) Yerman she can't abide. All the boys are off fighting these Yerman types, there's one right in the middle of us.

SALLY: There are old families of German descent here.

MATT: Ha-ha. You know nothing about dis Friedman. Might be anybody. Dis enemy maybe infiltrate de home front, ja?

SALLY: Don't. That's creepy.

MATT: You should only know. So! She does not think of Matt as a German. (*Tears off another page, looks at the next*)

28

Then Matt says: (*Carefully*) This Sally puzzle. She's how old? (SALLY *freezes*) Stop looking at yourself, Matt. It is not just Matt she is not liking. She is *well over* how old? All her friends and all her relatives were married by what age? And with all the prospering young men down here, some—

SALLY: All the prospering young men are off to war, Matt.

MATT: I think we are getting somewhere. Well, then all the handsome and pathetic and brave soldiers at the hospital she sees every day.

SALLY: They're kids. They're ten years younger than me; more, most of them.

MATT: This has got to be the most particular girl that ever was. Whoever heard of such a situation? Where is her bright-red hair net? Where're the rolled garters on her legs to drive men out of their mind. Why isn't she exposing half her bosom with a plunging neckline like every other female? Where is the come-hither? The invitation? (*Moves to* SALLY) Here is an un-married, attractive, not fanatically religious young lady who ac-tually thinks of herself as a human being rather than a feather-bed. And you say there is no mystery? Also, I talked to the patients at the hospital, remember? Some are not so young. And they all say, "Are you Sally's beau? Every time we say something sweet to Sally, try to get fresh, she says, Come on, now, I got a beau."

SALLY: (*A long pause. She is trying to speak and can't. After two attempts she says shakily*) There's time . . . enough . . . for . . .

MATT: (*Pause. Quietly*) It's just a friendly conversation, Sally. No reason to be upset.

SALLY: Oh, come . . . on. My life is no concern to you. If we get through the war, there's time to think about the future.

MATT: Nobody thinks like that any more. Live for today.

SALLY: Everything is upside down.

MATT: (*Turns her to face him*) No, no. We're not waiting for when Johnny comes marching home this time.

SALLY: I can't hear a word you're saying. You have a thing of blood on your face.

MATT: (*Alarmed. A spot of blood from a scratch has appeared over one eye*) Blood? Where? How did I get?

SALLY: You said that junk fell on you. Don't touch it. Don't— just put both your hands down. (*She takes a handkerchief from her purse, and a bottle from a hiding place. Lights a lantern, and hands it to him*) Hold this.

MATT: (*Looking at bottle, as she dabs handkerchief*) What is that?

SALLY: Never you mind.

MATT: What is that? (*She dabs at his forehead*) Ai! That stings. What are you putting on . . . ?

SALLY: Gin. You're not hurt; don't faint. Sit down.

MATT: I'm inoculated; it won't give me lockjaw.

SALLY: I'm sorry to hear it.

MATT: I had a tetanus shot. Ouch.

SALLY: I know. Because you read in a book how to be a fisherman.

MATT: (*As she chases him*) Some skills have to be acquired, you know. Man is not born with a knowledge of the river or nobody would ever drown. Ouch! This is a professional nurse's aide's bedside manner? Also, I read. In my business I had to learn to read very fast because they change the tax laws every week.

SALLY: (*A last dab at him*) One more.

MATT: So now I read like a madman, and I retain nothing at all. But I read like lightning.

SALLY: I read very slowly and practically memorize every word.

MATT: Jack Sprat. Am I okay?

SALLY: You'll live. (*She takes a nip from the bottle and passes it to him. He takes a drink, reacts, hands the bottle back.*)

MATT: You have Sen-Sen for your breath? (*She opens her purse*) No, no. (*He takes a cigarette, offers her one. She sighs, takes it. He gets a lighter from his pocket. It doesn't work. She opens her purse, produces a lighter, and lights his and hers. Looking around*) Poor Whistler. He should see what is happening to his boathouse. He'd sing "Una furtiva Lagrima."

SALLY: I used to think that he made the place for me. I was little when he died, but I thought he knew I'd come along, so he built it just the way it is—falling down—the way people used to build Roman ruins for their gardens. That way nobody else would come here and discover the magic of the place except me.

MATT: It was falling down? Even then?

SALLY: Well, it wasn't that long ago. I played in it when I was eight or ten, I'm twenty-seven now, so—

MATT: No, you're counting wrong.

SALLY: I'm what?

MATT: You're thirty-one.

SALLY: I am certainly not thirty-one. Who do—

MATT: Oh, my goodness. She does have a vanity as well as a temper. You are thirty-one because you were fired from teaching Sunday school on your twenty-eighth birthday and that's three years ago.

SALLY: What?

MATT: I've become great friends with your Aunt Charlotte. There's a counterspy in your very home. You're infiltrated. I didn't tell you. You're ambushed. I've come up on you from behind.

SALLY: When did you talk to Aunt Charlotte?

MATT: Last year. For a second today. And every few weeks during the winter. On the telephone. (*He laughs*) I had never heard of anyone being fired from Sunday school before.

SALLY: I quit, we didn't get along.

MATT: I like it better the way she told me. The preacher told you you were supposed to be teaching from the Methodist reader, not from Thorstein Veblen.

SALLY: They were having problems with union organizers at the garment factory.

MATT: Some of the kids' mothers work there.

SALLY: They asked me what was happening.

MATT: I like that. So you read to them from . . . ?

SALLY: *The Theory of the Leisure Class.*

MATT: How much of the garment factory does your family own?

SALLY: Almost twenty-five percent. Dad and the minister and the newspaper editor suggested we all concentrate on the text: "And he who does not work, neither shall he eat."

MATT: And scare the pants off the sluggards.

SALLY: Make the unreligious infidels buckle down.

MATT: Be good Christian workers.

SALLY: I also read from St. Augustine.

MATT: "Profit is a sin."

SALLY: "Businessmen will never enter the Kingdom."

MATT: He was also a terrible anti-Semite.

SALLY: Worse, he was Catholic.

MATT: Sally, you know that unmarried daughters are supposed to help the menfolk keep the social status quo.

SALLY: Organize food baskets for the poor.

MATT: Keep their mouths shut.

SALLY: There was a time when Dad had great hopes for me.

MATT: No wonder they are so eager to get you out of their house.

SALLY: You're older than I am.

MATT: Oh, more than you know. I'm forty-two.

SALLY: That's about what I imagined.

MATT: Sally, you don't say that. Whatever you think.

SALLY: Under the draft by the skin of your teeth.

MATT: Yes.

SALLY: You could have volunteered.

MATT: Yes.

SALLY: You've been married?

MATT: No, ma'am.

SALLY: Why?

MATT: Never asked anybody. Nobody ever asked me.

SALLY: You should have heard the other nurse's aides, after you left. They thought you were the bee's knees.

MATT: They still say that down here?

SALLY: They still say cat's pajamas. Only something is wrong. Something is goofy, isn't it? A single man, forty-two years old. It doesn't make sense that a good man hasn't made a fool of himself at least once by your age.

33

MATT: Well, puzzles. Why does the chicken cross the road? A man I know says some riddle to me every day. I say, Don't tell me, don't tell me. Later in the day I say, Okay, I give up. Puzzles and jokes.

SALLY: They couldn't quite put you together so they decided you weren't quite right. Maybe you had a wife and six kids in Germany.

MATT: You like jokes? Old Ben Franklin was standing at the kitchen window one morning flying his kite out the window. And his missus, Mrs. Franklin, comes in, looks out at the kite, and says to Ben, "You need more tail." (SALLY *reacts*) And Ben says to her: "That's what I told you this morning. And you told me to go fly a kite."

SALLY: I heard that before I was twelve.

MATT: I hadn't heard that before. Mrs. Blumenfeld in the office told us that yesterday morning.

SALLY: English wasn't your first language. What was?

MATT: Questions and answers. What is the shortest month? May is the shortest month, there are only three letters in May.

SALLY: German? Yiddish?

MATT: What was Matthew's first language? It doesn't come out funny. What does it matter; he can't talk to the old man at the cafeteria in Lithuanian any more. Not the way he would like to. Some. Pieces: "The weather is hot today." "Yes, the weather is hot. I read the Germans marched into Russia." "Yes, what happened to the German-Russian friendship, ho, ho, ho?" I yell to him like he was deaf.

SALLY: Where were you born?

MATT: I don't know.

SALLY: Where was the sidewalk they skated on?

MATT: (*Almost abrupt*) I lived in many cities. (*Sighs, maybe sits, or walks around*) Oh, dear. We are a lot alike, you know?

To be so different. We are two such private people. A guy the other day—I eat at this cafeteria, I talk to a lot of nutty guys—

SALLY: I don't want to hear another story, I—

MATT: No, no, no, this is not like that. I came down here to tell you this. This guy told me we were eggs.

SALLY: Who? You and me?

MATT: All people. He said people are eggs. Said we had to be careful not to bang up against each other too hard. Crack our shells, never be any use again. Said we were eggs. Individuals. We had to keep separate, private. He was very protective of his shell. He said nobody ever knows what the other guy is thinking. We all got about ten tracks going at once, nobody ever knows what's going down any given track at any given moment. So we never can really communicate. As I'm talking to you on track number three, over on track five I might be thinking about . . . (*Puts his hand on her back*) Oh, any number of things. (*Really asking*) And when I think you're listening to me, what are you really thinking?

SALLY: (*Removes his hand*) And you think he's right or you think he's wrong?

MATT: Well, that's two ways of looking at it. I told him he was paranoid. Ought not to worry too much about being understood. Ought to work at it. We . . . (*Puts his hand on her knee*) Got our work cut out for us, don't we? I told him . . .

SALLY: (*Gently pushes his hand away, and crosses her legs*) What?

MATT: (*Up and pacing*) Well, it's all right there in his analogy, ain't it? What good is an egg? Gotta be hatched or boiled or beat up into something like a lot of other eggs. Then you're cookin'. I told him he ought not to be too afraid of gettin' his yolk broke.

SALLY: Where were you born?

MATT: He didn't appreciate it either.

SALLY: Why are you being such a private person? Such an egg?

MATT: (*His back to us, staring out*) Where was Matt born? Uh, Rostock maybe or Dansk or Kaunas, but probably Kaunas, which became the capital of . . .

SALLY: Lithuania.

MATT: What *was* Lithuania. (*Turning*) So! There! Omelette!

SALLY: When did you come to America?

MATT: This is one you haven't heard; this is a city joke. The Kaiser's architect had a little outhouse he wanted plastered and painted, so he asked for bids from three contractors: a Polish man, an Italian, and a Jew.

SALLY: Matt—

MATT: So first the Pole says, Well, that job will cost you three thousand marks. Kaiser's architect says, How do you figure that? The Pole says, One thousand for the plasterer, one thousand for the painter, and one thousand for me. So the Italian says, That will be six thousand marks. Kaiser's architect says, How is that six thousand marks? The Italian says, Two thousand for the plasterer, two thousand for the painter, two thousand for me. So he goes to the Jewish contractor and he says, That job will be nine thousand marks. Nine thousand marks! How can you figure that? So the Jew says, Three thousand for you, three thousand for me, and three thousand for the Pole.

SALLY: You said you were German, why were you born in Lithuania?

MATT: Probably Lithuania.

SALLY: Did you come here with your family? (*Pause*) To this country? (*Pause*) Or don't you know that either.

MATT: I know, I know. (*Pause. Finally decides*) Very well, Miss Sally Talley. There was a Prussian and a Uke (Ukrainian, yes?). A Prussian and a Uke and a Lat and a Probable Lit, who all traveled over Europe.

36

SALLY: Matt, you're maddening—I don't know if this is a story or a—

MATT: I will tell this, Sally, in the only way I can tell it. The Prussian had been a soldier, but then he realized that, being Jewish, he could not advance in the Kaiser's army, so then he became an engineer.

SALLY: There's no such thing as a Prussian Jew.

MATT: (*Rather Prussian*) Prussian is the way the Prussian thought of himself, and Prussian he was. (*She sighs, perhaps says, "Very well"*) So he became a Wandering . . . Engineer. The Kaiser sent the Prussian and the Uke and the Lat and the Probable Lit to study engineering wonders: many months in the Swiss mountains to watch the building of a funicular, yes?

SALLY: Yes.

MATT: And in the evening the Prussian liked to sit stiffly and talk with other stiff Prussian Jews sitting around the cafés of the capitals of Europe. But unfortunately, one of the people with whom the Prussian spoke was—

SALLY: Matt, you're confusing me and I don't know if this is a joke or this is—

MATT: This is the joke about how the Probable Lit came to America that you said you wanted to hear. So one of the people with whom he spoke was an inventor named—who remembers—such is fame—who had discovered how to get nitrogen out of air. Like magic. So one day the Prussian and the Uke and the Lat and the Probable Lit lit out for Naples but were detained in Nice, where there is a large police force, because people try to board boats there to cross borders, Europe being mostly made up of borders that people get upset when you try to cross. Europe is the child's game of May I. You know May I? "Captain, may I cross into Yugoslavia?" "Yes, you may take three scissor steps." "Okay, I take three scissor steps." "Oh, oh, go back to Czechoslovakia. You forgot to say, 'May I.' "

SALLY: Who is the Uke and who is the Lat? You're the Lit and the Prussian is your father? Who is the Uke?

MATT: This is all on the up-and-up, Sally, the Prussian was married to the Uke. She said she was Sephardic, but that wasn't true.

SALLY: (*Knows somehow that he is talking about something important*) Okay. I want to understand this, Matt. Who was the Lat?

MATT: The Lat was their daughter, who had been born in Latvia two years before the Probable Lit had been born probably in Lithuania.

SALLY: I didn't know you have a sister.

MATT: (*Looking across the river. Low*) It turned out to be of little consequence, people in Europe being very wasteful of people.

SALLY: (*Beat*) And your family was detained in Nice?

MATT: Yes, by the Nice police. Which was very unlucky, as the French are very much the natural enemy of the Prussians, and the French very much wanted to know from the Prussian engineer . . . What? (*Beat*) Something he had overheard in a café.

SALLY: (*Long pause. Troubled answer*) How to get nitrogen from the air.

MATT: Like magic!

SALLY: Why?

MATT: Everyone was happily looking forward to the Great War.

SALLY: This was when?

MATT: This was 1911, the Lit was nine. And this nitrogen is not used in the fields as fertilizer. This nitrogen is used in the manufacture of gunpowder. So one should be very careful what your friends tell you in cafés. (*This is difficult to say, and there is a bitterness underlying it which he does not show*) So the French torture the Prussian—

SALLY: Oh, no—

MATT: Who, being Prussian and Jewish, says nothing, and the French decide to torture the Lat daughter to make the Prussian speak.

SALLY: Matt, you don't have to say anything, I know—

MATT: The consequences being that the Lat fell into a coma from which she did not recover and the French were convinced that they had the wrong Prussian, Uke, Lat, and Lit, and let the whole lot of them go. So they went to the authorities in Germany, leaving the little Lit with his uncle in Lübeck. The irony turned out to be that the German government reasoned that this gregarious Prussian engineer knew something vital to the interest of the Kaiser—

SALLY: Oh, no—

MATT: Well, as he did. So the Prussian and the Uke tried to slip across the border into Denmark. But, we understand, they forgot to say, "May I?"

SALLY: They wouldn't kill their own people just because they knew something they might or might not tell—

MATT: —Well, they didn't consider them their own, of course. And people were not killed in Germany. They were indefinitely detained.

SALLY: I never heard that there were persecutions in the First World War.

MATT: I thought you said you reread the Old Testament.

SALLY: How did he get to America? The Lit?

MATT: Who said the little Lit came to America?

SALLY: How did he get to America?

MATT: Norway to Caracas to America on a banana boat.

SALLY: By himself? Or with refugees?

MATT: Refugees, smefugees. With the uncle from Lübeck and his wife and four kids.

SALLY: Little kids?

MATT: What does it matter what size kids? No. Grown people. Not little kids. There is always something thrilling about the broad canvas of a European story, isn't there? (*Pause*) But I am afraid that the Probable Lit had seen too much. No allegiances would claim him any more, no causes.

SALLY: So the Lit didn't volunteer for the army.

MATT: Oh, war. What did he know except war; life was war, war was life. Against the French he would almost have gone this time. No. (*Looking at her*) The resolve was never to be responsible for bringing into such a world another living soul. He would not bring into this world another child to be killed for a political purpose. This boy knew blank about sitting alone without a woman to talk to. (*Pause*) So the little Lit was a little crazy, and I'm afraid as he grew older he got a little crazier, but he has witnessed nothing to cause him to alter his conviction. (*Watching her closely*) And what woman would be interested in such a grown Probable Lit with such a resolve? (*Pause. She doesn't answer*) Anyway, he doesn't think about it. The day is over in a second. I spend my life adding figures. It breaks my head.

SALLY: (*Very level*) He does. The Lit.

MATT: Does what?

SALLY: You said "I." You mean the Lit. The Lit spends his life adding figures.

MATT: Yes, well, I do too. We are much alike. We work together.

SALLY: You've both gone to a lot of work for nothing.

MATT: What work? What do you mean?

SALLY: Or do you naturally invent stories about your sister and father and mother being killed by Germans?

MATT: One by the French; two by the Germans.

SALLY: You've been talking to Aunt Lottie? Who else have you talked to? People in town? Have you looked in the Lebanon newspaper? The old files? I don't know how detectives work.

MATT: This is bad. Why are you speaking like this?

SALLY: Why did you tell me that story?

MATT: To make you see why I had not spoken last year.

SALLY: That's what you came down here to tell me?

MATT: Yes.

SALLY: Well, now you've told me. Now I know. Now you can leave.

MATT: (*Worried*) I have said something I don't know that I have said.

SALLY: (*She hurries to leave*) It was a calculated risk; you just miscalculated. (*Hides the gin, grabs her jacket and purse*) You're not good at manipulation. I've been worked over by experts. (*Blows out the lantern*) They're good down here. (*The boathouse is flooded in moonlight*)

MATT: Sally, you have mistaken something—

SALLY: —Get gone now. Leave before I hit you with something. You can walk to the Barnettes', they'll give you some gas for a couple of coupons.

MATT: Now who is making the disturbance?

SALLY: (*Angry; quite loud*) Get off this property or get out of my way so I can go back to the house, or I'll disturb you for real.

MATT: We are going to settle this before anyone goes anywhere.

SALLY: I won't be made a fool just because I fell in love again, Matt, and I won't be pushed around again.

MATT: You're not getting away from me.

SALLY: Get out of here!

MATT: Do you realize what you said? Did you hear yourself?

SALLY: (*Yelling toward the door*) Buddy! Cliffy! Here he is. Matt Friedman is down here! (*Her last words are muffled by* MATT's *hand as he grabs her and holds her fast. She tries to speak over his lines*)

MATT: (*Grabbing her*) Vilde chaya! You are a crazy woman! We could both be shot with that gun. People do not scream and yell and kick. (*She stops struggling*) People are blessed with the beautiful gift of reason and communication. (*He starts to release her*)

SALLY: Cliffy!

MATT: (*Grabbing her again*) How can such a thing happen? When they passed out logic everybody in the Ozarks went on a marshmallow roast. You are rational now? (*He releases her. She moves away,* MATT *stands where he can block her exit*) Life is going to be interesting with you. You're hurt?

SALLY: No.

MATT: My hand is bleeding. Where did you hide the alcohol? (*He goes to the gin bottle, keeping an eye on her*) I called my uncle and my aunt. Seventy years old. They say, Matt, don't get mixed up with the *goyim*. They have my cousins call me; old neighbors I haven't heard from in years. I say I must live my own life. I come down here protected from tetanus; I am getting rabies from an *alte moid*.

SALLY: (*Level*) Why did you tell me about your family, and about you?

MATT: (*Pouring the gin on his hand*) Because you asked me. Why have you not married? Where were you born? How did you get to this stupid country? Because I am a crazy person. Your nurse friends all say something is wacky with Matt that he has never made a fool of himself over some woman; I said, Matt, go down, tell Sally who you are. Once in your life *risk* something. At least you will know that you did what you could. What do you think she is going to do, bite you?

SALLY: (*Pause*) Charlotte told you nothing. She may be silly. She may like you.

MATT: One does not necessarily follow the other.

SALLY: But she doesn't gossip about me. She didn't tell you anything.

MATT: So you tell me. No, Charlotte told me nothing except that there was something to tell. I said, Charlotte, Sherlock thinks that there is some dark mystery down here and Charlotte said, Mr. Holmes, Sally will have to tell you that herself.

SALLY: There is nothing to tell.

MATT: You were screaming up to the house for the sheriff because there is—Oh, my— (*Listens*) They could all be coming down here now.

SALLY: They're all listening to the radio.

MATT: Saved by Miss Fanny Brice. We stick together. Oh, my gosh! I do not know how to begin! I am walking into an unfriendly church in my underdrawers, here.

SALLY: What are you talking about?

MATT: You don't have that dream? I congratulate you. That is a terrible dream. I mean, I am at such a disadvantage here. (*With an energy born from frustration*) None of my skills is appropriate to the situation I find myself in. And I have amazing skills. I could be an attraction in a sideshow. Give me a list of three, six, up to fifteen numbers, five digits each, I'll tell you the sum immediately. In my head, Mr. Adding Machine. Ev-

43

erybody gapes. How does he do that? He's got it all written down. I know the multiplication table up to seventy-five times seventy-five. Truly. It's something I know. What is sixty-seven times sixty-eight? Four thousand five hundred fifty-six. I have amazing skills. Only I feel like Houdini in the iron box under the ice at the bottom of the river. I forgot where I put the key to the handcuffs. Such a frustrating dream.

SALLY: One of the boys at the hospital is an artist. He's developed a facility for when a dream starts to go bad. It starts to get scary. He, in the dream, changes it all into a drawing, wads it up, and throws it away.

MATT: Freud wouldn't like it.

SALLY: Oh, drive him crazy.

MATT: I am foolish to insinuate myself down here and try to feel like one of the hillbillies. Who ever heard of this Friedman? I don't blame you. I won't be Matt Friedman any more. I'll join the throng. Call myself . . . August Hedgepeth. Sip moonshine over the back of my elbow. Wheat straw in the gap in my teeth. I'm not cleaning my glasses, I'm fishing for crappie. Bass.

SALLY: Sun perch.

MATT: Oh, heck yes. Only I'm not. I can't even take off my shoes without feeling absurd.

SALLY: People don't walk around with their shoes off here, sipping moonshine. It isn't really the Hatfields and the McCoys. The ones who go barefoot only do it because they can't afford shoes, Matt . . . I . . .

MATT: Matt? Who's that? I don't even hear you. My name is August. Call me August.

SALLY: I couldn't possibly.

MATT: That's my name as of this minute.

SALLY: Matt, you—

MATT: Who? Huh? Wha?

SALLY: (*A pause. Finally*) August . . .

MATT: I don't like it. What is that fragrance? What are you wearing?

SALLY: It isn't me.

MATT: Smell.

SALLY: Honeysuckle.

MATT: That's honeysuckle? No wonder they make songs about it. It blooms at night?

SALLY: No, that's something else. It blooms during the day, the night, whenever.

MATT: It's wonderful.

SALLY: You've never had to grub it out of a garden.

MATT: You know that folk song? (*Sings*) "Lindy, did you smell that honeysuckle vine last night? Honey, it was smellin' so sweet in de moonlight."

SALLY: No. I mean sure, but I don't know it.

MATT: We heard the Lebanon band play it last summer. Isn't that a Missouri folk song?

SALLY: No. I don't know. I don't know Missouri folk songs.

MATT: (*Sings*) "Oh, God, I'd lay me down and die, If I could be as sweet as that to you." (*Directly to her, low and trying to sing well*) "Oooooo-oooooo. My little Lindy Lou . . ."

SALLY: Don't sing to me, it's ridiculous. And my name is not Lindy Lou. It's Sally Talley. (*They both smile*)

MATT: I know, I came down to talk to you about that.

SALLY: Well, I'm not going to change— (*Dead stop. Count fifteen*)

45

MATT: Why is your chin trembling? You okay? Sally?

SALLY: You didn't say that. Don't say that.

MATT: It's what I want to say.

SALLY: Well, don't. Talk about your socialism, talk about your work or something, like you did in your letters.

MATT: I don't talk Socialism, I don't talk Communism, I talk common sense. I don't think much of isms. In no time at all you start defending isms like they were something tangible. What are you afraid of? Why—

SALLY: (*Cutting him off*) And that's what made Buddy so angry? And Olive? Talking common sense?

MATT: No, your brother is a baiter. You want to change the subject? Fine.

SALLY: A what?

MATT: (*Almost angry*) A baiter! A baiter. He baits people. Buddy thinks that if all the factory workers went on strike for better wages, as they are trying to do in his factory, it would bring the country to its knees. He is a very poetic speaker.

SALLY: Well, it would bring Buddy to his knees, and that's a position with which he is very unfamiliar, believe me.

MATT: What are you afraid of?

SALLY: People are working now at least.

MATT: Economics, you want to talk? I say to you: This is my life. This is what I want. Say no or say yes, and you say: Talk about economics?

SALLY: Will there really be strikes after the war is over?

MATT: (*Glares at her*) You are playing games, yes?

SALLY: I don't know what—

MATT: You are a peach. After the war they'll strike, yes. People say. Shaking in their boots. Sure. They'll strike. Everybody from soda jerks to grease monkeys. It gives them the illusion that the system is working.

SALLY: (*Also worried. Trying one more diversion*) People are afraid to admit it, but I think they're worried about what's going to happen when the boys come back.

MATT: (*Increasingly angry*) Down here they're afraid to admit it? I'm glad to hear it. It shows humility. Humility is good for the soul. In St. Louis they tremble in their beds at night. Headlines in the papers. One businessman said the war had to last another two years or the nation would never recover.

SALLY: They're afraid that there will be another Depression.

MATT: They who?

SALLY: They. They. Who do we ever mean when we say they?

MATT: Man I know says, "They-sayers are all liars."

SALLY: They see it happening all over again: the Depression, unemployment, with the factories shut down, higher taxes.

MATT: No.

SALLY: What do you mean, no?

MATT: No. It won't happen.

SALLY: You can't know that.

MATT: There is a lot I do not know. On people I am utterly ignorant. On girls I am more than ignorant. On money I am an expert only. On taxes I am an authority. Businesses ask *me* about taxes. People who cry depression are blind and frightened.

SALLY: Why should it be different this time?

MATT: You are worried? About what is going to be?

SALLY: Yes. It was no fun. Hobos coming up to the back door four and five at a time. Every day. Asking for work and having to accept handouts.

MATT: It's different. It won't be like that again. Roosevelt him-self will be the one passing out lollipops.

SALLY: I don't know why you're acting like this. All I—

MATT: How much money do you have?

SALLY: What?

MATT: (*Furious*) You're an average person in a less-than-average job. You've been working only two and a half, three years. How much money do you have saved? You have nothing to spend it on, you put it in a savings account, you buy bonds to save capitalism, excuse me, democracy—er—a—freedom of speech, were you not terrified to express yourself—how much have you saved?

SALLY: What's wrong? I'm not going to let you talk to—

MATT: Forget it. How much?

SALLY: (*Beat*) I do know how much money I've saved. That's what bothers me. Money makes me greedy and guilty at the same time.

MATT: So how much?

SALLY: Half my check every week for three years. I make thirty dollars a week.

MATT: Twenty-three hundred forty dollars!

SALLY: A little less. Twenty-two hundred.

MATT: Multiply that times one hundred twenty million people.

SALLY: You're the mathematician, what does it come to?

MATT: A lot of money. That nobody had before the war. Burning a hole in everybody's pockets. How many people have bought war bonds? Eighty-five million people! How much money is in savings banks? One hundred thirty billion dollars! Everybody is going to be spending and building and working.

48

The sideshow is over! End of financial exhibition. I'll go. Why did I come? You aren't going to be honest with me.

SALLY: Honest about what?

MATT: About you, about me, about Sally and Matt. You think I intend to sit here and talk finance? What will happen after the war. Why should there be an after-the-war?

SALLY: I was being perfectly honest with you.

MATT: Perfectly honest and perfectly evasive. Perfectly mysterious and perfectly frightened out of your wits. (*Bogart*) "You know somethin', baby? You dames are all alike. Ya yella. Ya all got a yella streak a mile wide right down the middle of ya back."

SALLY: Is that supposed to be Cagney?

MATT: (*Crushed*) No; oh, my goodness! Cagney! That's still Bogart. You have no sense of flattery.

SALLY: And we're all yella. You know that many women, you can make a generalization like that?

MATT: Oh, good grief. Now what are you going to be? Jealous and possessive about something you don't even want? No. I know no women. What I told you I have never before spoken for the same reason that you speak nothing to anybody, because we are terrified that if once we allow ourselves to be cracked—I think people really do think that they're eggs. They're afraid they are the—who is the eggman, all the king's horses and—

SALLY: Humpty Dumpty.

MATT: We all have a Humpty Dumpty complex. So now I take a big chance. I come down here to tell you I am in love for the only time in my life with a girl who sees the world exactly as I see it. I say to you, I am sorry, Sally, I will not have children, but if there is a life for the two of us, will you have me or not? You scream and yell bloody murder, you kick, you

49

—ah, breathe fast, what do you call it, breathing fast in and out, in and out—?

SALLY: Hyperventilate.

MATT: You hyperventilate and say, Matthew, talk about finance. (*Sighs*) Oh, boy, oh, boy.

SALLY: (*A long pause*) You can come with me to the road. I'll get you some gas. I'll go into the yard by myself.

MATT: The car isn't out of gas.

SALLY: (*Beat*) What is it out of?

MATT: Hope! The car is out of hope. The car is in fine running condition. I turn the key, it goes; I turn it off, it stops. I turned it off. I didn't say it was out of gas, I said it needs gas to run. You assumed it was out of gas. (*Pause*) I wasn't talking to Buddy about isms up at the house, I was telling him about you and me down here in the boathouse last summer.

SALLY: Oh, my God! Oh!

MATT: Hey, come on, you'll drown out Fibber McGee.

SALLY: You didn't!

MATT: They'll arrest us both. Shhhh! They'll hear you swear right across the river at the park. You want to hear the band play in Whistler's band shell? So the night shouldn't be a waste?

SALLY: You didn't.

MATT: They ought to start any time. We can watch the fireworks.

SALLY: They won't have fireworks; you can hear the band from here. Matt, you have no idea how prejudiced Buddy and Olive are! Really!

MATT: You kidding me? I don't imagine your father will let you sleep under his roof after Buddy tells them. Your aunt thought it was very likely you'd be kicked out of the house. We think maybe they'll shave your head.

SALLY: Aunt Lottie put you up to this?

MATT: She said you were anxious to get out of the house, but you didn't have much courage. She is a very bold strategist.

SALLY: You told her about last summer?

MATT: No, she told me. You told Rachel, Rachel told her cousin Rose, Rose told your Aunt Charlotte.

SALLY: I'll brain them, every one.

MATT: You been listening to anything I've said?

SALLY: What? Oh, Matt, I told you, put it out of your head.

MATT: You're hard. You're tough.

SALLY: Well, I can't think about it now.

MATT: Maybe you better.

SALLY: There is no place to go or I'd be out of there, Matt.

MATT: There's a hospital in St. Louis. St. Ann's. St. Louis's St. Ann's. Where you could work. They're crying for help.

SALLY: Too long a drive.

MATT: Well, it happens my apartment is conveniently located four blocks away.

SALLY: You have room for three nurse's aides?

MATT: I rescind the offer. You like St. Louis? The Browns, you never know. The Cardinals are okay. We can go to the game, watch the Cooper brothers.

SALLY: Matt, you can see I don't want you to talk like that.

MATT: I hear you say that. I think I see something different. You aren't afraid of me. This minute, are you afraid of me right now?

SALLY: I've never been afraid of you.

MATT: Put everything I've said behind. I didn't sing "Lindy Lou" and ask Sally to marry me. Sally didn't say, Don't sing. We are friends talking together, looking at the river and the upside-down black trees with the shaky moon in the water. (*Suddenly noticing*) Hey! There's no color. In moonlight. What a gyp. Very little color. Look at you.

SALLY: (*Looks at him*) Some.

MATT: You might as well have blue eyes. Amazing the things you get so used to that you don't know them any more. Okay. So I ask you. Why did your aunt say, "There is something you don't know, Matt, and something only Sally can tell you"?

SALLY: It was a long time ago.

MATT: You're thirty-one years old. How long—

SALLY: It was another life, really—

MATT: So what happened in this other life?

SALLY: Say I was disappointed in love. It was a long time ago. I was another person.

MATT: No, I don't believe in disappointed in love.

SALLY: It was more of a financial arrangement than anything.

MATT: Oh, well. Disappointed in a financial arrangement, I understand.

SALLY: I was engaged to Harley Campbell, his dad owned—

MATT: I don't believe it.

SALLY: You don't even know who he is.

MATT: I met him up at the house. He was the one that was saying, "You tell 'em, Buddy. You tell 'em, Buddy."

SALLY: Well, he used to be very good-looking.

MATT: I don't believe that either.

SALLY: (*Not rhapsodic; detached, but this is an unpleasant memory*) He was a guard on the basketball team; I was a cheerleader. We grew up together. We were the two richest families in town. We were golden children. Dad owned a quarter of the garment factory; Harley's dad owned a third. These two great families were to be united in one happy factory. We used to walk through the plant holding hands, waving at all the girls; they loved us. When the workers asked for a showdown to discuss their demands, Dad brought us right into the meeting, onto the platform. Everybody applauded.

MATT: The youth, the beauty . . .

SALLY: The money. Here they are, folks. The future of the country. Do you love them or do you love them? Now back to work. They still don't have a union.

MATT: So how did it happen that Sally was disappointed in love?

SALLY: It all became academic. The Depression happened. Maybe we didn't look so golden. The factory almost closed.

MATT: I know the Depression came. So how did it happen that Sally was disappointed in love?

SALLY: (*With some difficulty*) I was sick for a long time. I got TB and missed school. I didn't graduate until a year after Harley did. It was a good excuse to drift apart. (*Easier*) Then he went to Princeton, became engaged to a girl from New Jersey, his father killed himself.

MATT: Because he was engaged to a girl from New Jersey?

SALLY: Because by then it was 1931. He was in debt. He thought he would lose the factory. He didn't know how to live poor.

MATT: So?

SALLY: Harley quit school, Buddy and Harley and Dad worked at the factory, trying to save it. They're doing fine now.

MATT: I know. A government contract for army uniforms. So?

SALLY: Harley's wife left him eight years ago; he remarried a girl from Rogersville.

MATT: (*Looks at her a moment*) So that's the truth, the whole truth, and nothing but the truth, so help you, Hannah.

SALLY: Yes.

MATT: You're real cute. (*Pause*) Might as well get the gas, don't you think?

SALLY: You're not out of gas.

MATT: Yes, maybe I am. Maybe I lied.

SALLY: Well, if that's what it takes.

MATT: You know what I'm thinking? Over on track number nine? That Sally may not be who I thought she was, after all.

SALLY: Maybe not.

MATT: May not be. Maybe not. What kind of an answer to a mystery is that? What happened to change this Golden Girl into an embarrassment to the family? Into a radical old maid who is fired from teaching Sunday school? Why would this nice Harley leave you after all this time while you were sick with such a romantic disease? See, I'm a logical person. I have to have it all laid out like in a list, and that isn't logical.

SALLY: His family didn't want him to marry me, obviously.

MATT: They thought you weren't good enough for him?

SALLY: Come on. (*As she starts to move past him to the door, he reaches out and takes her wrist. The band, rather distant, plays a fanfare*)

MATT: What?

SALLY: Yes. Don't do that.

54

MATT: Mr. Campbell was in debt and worried about being overextended, but the rich partner's daughter gets TB and the wedding is off?

SALLY: I don't know.

MATT: There's your music. Wasn't Harley the richest boy in town, you said?

SALLY: Yes.

MATT: And Sally was the richest girl in the countryside. This was the match of the decade. Bells were going to ring for such a match.

SALLY: Well, they didn't.

MATT: When the Depression comes, rich families must pool their resources.

SALLY: They didn't see it that way.

MATT: The Campbells are a large Missouri family, are they? Fifteen little Campbells?

SALLY: No.

MATT: No. Only Harley, two brothers, and one sister?

SALLY: No.

MATT: Only Harley and his brother?

SALLY: Harley and his sister.

MATT: Harley was the only son of a very prominent Laclede County family.

SALLY: Yes.

MATT: So why didn't they want their only son to marry the beautiful, popular, cheerleader Talley girl whom he had been going steady with for three years?

SALLY: They didn't like me.

MATT: All those years he dated you over their protest?

SALLY: Not on your life.

MATT: No, because Harley did not do things against his parents' wishes.

SALLY: No.

MATT: But in fact you didn't graduate with Harley. You were delayed a full year.

SALLY: That's beginning to hurt, Matt.

MATT: You're pulling, I'm not pulling. (*Releases her, but stands in her path*) Why weren't you good enough for Harley?

SALLY: I got sick.

MATT: You got TB and went to Arizona, where you lived for the rest of your life.

SALLY: No.

MATT: You gave this contagious disease to their only son and he went away to Arizona and was never heard from again.

SALLY: The TB was not serious. There were complicating circumstances that caused me to be out of school.

MATT: There were complications. Sally was pockmarked and ugly and nobody wanted anything to do with her.

SALLY: You might say that.

MATT: This only son was repulsed by the sight of you.

SALLY: No, Matt. I was in the hospital for a month. I had a fever.

MATT: This Harley has a morbid fear of hospitals. I'm getting a fever is who's getting a fever.

SALLY: They didn't want it.

MATT: But your dad insisted.

SALLY: He didn't want it either.

MATT: You were pale and white and would not look good in a wedding dress.

SALLY: Matt.

MATT: You were a tramp and a vamp and would have ruined the reputation of this prominent family. Is what the story is?

SALLY: He was the heir. He had to carry on the family name!

MATT: And you were irresponsible; you had uncontrollable kleptomania and could not be trusted around the family money.

SALLY: I was sick! I had a fever.

MATT: You were delirious and drunken and no family would allow such a woman to marry their only son.

SALLY: (*She tries to run past him*) I was sick for a year.

MATT: (*Holds her again*) You were not sick. You went away. Why did you go away?

SALLY: I was at the house.

MATT: (*Driving*) Why were you in the house for a year?

SALLY: I had a fever.

MATT: No. Because you had disgraced yourself.

SALLY: I had a pelvic infection.

MATT: Is that what you told people?

SALLY: They didn't know what was wrong with me.

MATT: Why were you hiding in the house?

SALLY: They couldn't get the fever down!

MATT: Why were you hiding?

SALLY: (*Hitting him*) They couldn't break the fever! By the time they did, it didn't matter.

MATT: What were you hiding—

SALLY: Because it had eaten out my insides! I couldn't bear children. I can't have children! Let go of me. (*She breaks away, crying, falls against something, and sits*)

MATT: What do you mean?

SALLY: I couldn't have children.

MATT: Sally, I'm here, you're okay. It's okay.

SALLY: Go away. Go away.

MATT: (*Sitting beside her*) I didn't know. I thought you had had a child.

SALLY: I have had no child. There was no scandal. I was no longer of value to the merger.

MATT: It's okay. It's okay.

SALLY: Oh, stop. That's what I tell the boys. It's okay. Only they're dying of blood poisoning. Don't comfort me. I'm fine. Blast you. Let go.

MATT: I thought you had had a child by someone else. You're so crazy.

SALLY: I only wish I had.

MATT: This was a result of the TB?

SALLY: (*She looks at him for a long moment. Then finally, no longer crying*) The infection descended into the fallopian tubes; it's not uncommon with women at all. And so there couldn't be an heir to the garment empire. (*Almost laughing*) It was all such a great dance. Everyone came to the hospital. Everyone said it made no difference. By the time Harley graduated, the Campbells weren't speaking to the Talleys. By then Dad was looking at me like I was a broken swing. It was a very interesting perspective.

MATT: Did you think that your aunt had told me you couldn't have children and I was making up the story of my life just to tease you?

SALLY: Possibly.

MATT: (*To the sky*) Eggs! Eggs! Eggs! Eggs! We're so terrified. But we still hope. You take a beautiful dress to work— Did you tell the nurses I was coming to see you?

SALLY: No!

MATT: And look at me. For five years I have been wearing the same tie to work. It is a matter of principle with me not to wear a different tie. I buy a new tie to come and see Sally. You see how corruption of principle begins.

SALLY: I had nothing to do with that.

MATT: Is that a new dress, by the way? I don't know that dress.

SALLY: Yes. It's no big deal.

MATT: It is an enormous deal! It is the new New Deal! It is a Big Deal!

SALLY: You didn't even say you liked it.

MATT: I like it, I love the dress. (*Pause*) I was sitting up in St. Louis all this winter in a terrible quandary. It is not that I have been happy or not happy, but that I have not thought that I *could* be happy. (*Beat*) But this winter I was terribly unhappy and I *knew* I was unhappy. I had fallen for a girl and could not give her the life she would surely expect, with a family, many children. (*Pause. Taking her hand*) You know what has happened? Some mischievous angel has looked down and saw us living two hundred miles apart and said, You know what would be a kick in the head? Let's send Matt on a vacation to Lebanon.

SALLY: You believe in angels?

59

MATT: I do now, most definitely. Her name might be Lottie Talley, maybe. (*Pause*) We missed your marching band.

SALLY: They'll play all evening.

MATT: (*Pause*) So. We'll go up to the city tonight. Leave the car here—

SALLY: Oh, Matt, it's absurd to be talking like that; we're practically middle-aged.

MATT: So. We'll go up to the city tonight. Leave the car in town, take the midnight bus.

SALLY: (*Pause*) I'll be up in a week or so.

MATT: (*Pause*) I'll stay here at the hotel in Lebanon and wait.

SALLY: You have to work tomorrow.

MATT: So what?

SALLY: (*Pause*) We'll go tonight. (*They kiss. The distant band strikes up a soft but lightly swinging rendition of "Lindy Lou." They laugh*)

MATT: "Lindy Lou." (*Pause. They are sitting holding hands, perfectly relaxed.* MATT *looks around*) You live in such a beautiful country. Such a beautiful countryside. Will you miss it?

SALLY: Yes.

MATT: Me too. Once a year we'll come back down, so we don't forget.

SALLY: All right.

MATT: (*Looks at her for a long while, then his gaze drifts to the audience*) And so, all's well that ends . . . (*Takes out his watch, shows time to* SALLY, *then to audience*) . . . right on the button. Good night. (*They embrace.*)

The song continues as the light fades